CHERRY LANE

HEAVY METAL
GUITAR METHOD

MODES
by Jon Chappell and Michael Wolfsohn

Cover Design: Kerstin Fairbend
Cover Photography: Frank White (concert), Robin Visotsky (black and white)
Book Design: Kerstin Fairbend
Music Engraving: Gordon Hallberg
Production Manager: Daniel Rosenbaum
Administration: Monica Corton
Director of Music: Mark Phillips

FINALE™ notation software was used to engrave the musical examples in this book.

ISBN: 0-89524-662-7

About This Series

The **Heavy Metal Guitar Method** is an exciting new series that teaches you how to play heavy metal guitar. Through this unique approach you will learn the basic skills common to all guitar playing, integrated with the special techniques essential for playing heavy metal music and achieving a metal sound.

Methods	*Companion Songbooks*
Primer*	Songbook I: Primer and Book One
Book One*	
Book Two*	Songbook II
Book Three*	Songbook III

Cassette Tape Available Separately

Supplementary Books

Modes
Chord Book
Right-Hand Tapping
Harmonics, Distortion and Feedback
The Whammy Bar & Other Right-Hand Techniques
Guitar FX and Signal Processors
Advanced Scales and Modes for Heavy Metal

About the Authors

Jon Chappell
Author and Series Editor

Michael Wolfsohn
Co-Author

After seeing the Beatles on the "Ed Sullivan Show," Jon Chappell knew it was time to quit piano lessons—and did so the following day. Thus began his lifelong addiction to guitar. After receiving a master's degree in music composition from DePaul University in Chicago, he worked as a teacher, arranger and studio musician. Since migrating to New York he has worked as a writer and arranger for major music publishers, and in 1989 became Associate Music Editor for Cherry Lane Music Company. He wears headphones often and resides in Rye, N.Y.

Michael Wolfsohn was born in Chicago in 1950. He began playing the piano at age eight, but soon discovered the guitar. During the '60s and '70s he developed an interest in rock, blues and many other styles of music, and learned to play several instruments. He has been playing, teaching and recording professionally since 1974, and currently lives and teaches in New York City.

CONTENTS

Introduction

Modes are used by all the modern metal masters, from Steve Vai to Joe Satriani to Metallica's Kirk Hammett. If you want to roam similar musical terrain, a working knowledge of modes is an absolute **must.**

Modes is a comprehensive guide to the seven basic modes: what they are, what they sound like, and how to use them. This book is designed for those who have mastered the **Cherry Lane Heavy Metal Guitar Method: Book One** or for guitarists at the intermediate level who have a basic understanding of music notation.

Part One: Modes Defined

SCALES, KEYS AND TONAL CENTERS

Each key, denoted by a letter name (E, A, D, etc.) and a quality (such as major or minor), is determined by its tonal center or "home" chord. The tonal center is like a magnet: it keeps drawing a melody or chord progression back toward it. Most songs end on the "home" chord.

Each key and its corresponding home chord are derived from a **scale**. A scale contains seven notes that are organized sequentially. To play a scale, start with the key's name-tone (the **tonic**) and play the note with the next letter name, then the next, and so on. After playing seven notes, you will again reach the tonic—one octave higher. Let's try this in the key of C major.

THE C MAJOR SCALE

Below is a one-octave C major scale. You could repeat these same notes above or below this octave and still form a C major scale, as long as the notes were played in exactly the same sequence. Remember, a scale is like a ladder: Each step must be taken in succession. Notes must be played in alphabetical order—no skips, no repeats.

WHOLE AND HALF STEPS

Scales are differentiated by their whole- and half-step patterns. A half step is the smallest musical interval (distance between two notes). On the guitar, a half step is the distance of one fret. In other words, if you play a note anywhere on the guitar, the note at the fret immediately above or below is a half step away.

In this example, the second note is a half step below the first note; the fourth note is a half step above the third.

It follows, then, that a whole step is the distance of two half steps (two frets on the guitar). For example:

The second note is a whole step below the first note; the fourth note is a whole step above the third.

■ THE MAJOR SCALE PATTERN

Now let's examine the C major scale in terms of whole steps and half steps.

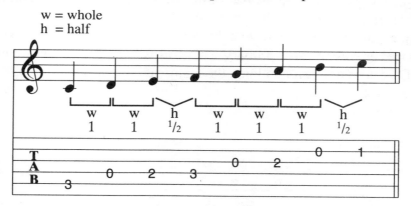

We find a pattern of two whole steps, a half step, three whole steps and a half step. This is the **major scale pattern**. If you follow this pattern starting from **any** note, you will play a major scale. Let's try this starting on G.

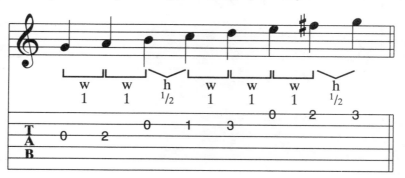

Remember, each letter name must occur in sequence, although some notes will have to be **sharped** or **flatted** to achieve the correct half- and whole-step pattern.

Now apply the major scale pattern starting on D.

Notice that each scale has the same sound relative to the first note (or tonic):
*the familiar **do-re-mi-fa-sol-la-ti-do** major scale sound.*

■ THE RELATIVE MINOR SCALE

The other primary scale found in a key system is the **natural minor scale** ("natural" because it occurs naturally in the key signature—no **chromatic alterations** are needed to produce this type of minor scale). If we take the notes from the C major scale and play them in the same scalar fashion (one after the other, alphabetically, with no skips or repeats) but start from the sixth degree of the scale, A, we get the natural minor scale for A. This is also called the **relative minor scale** of C major because it contains exactly the same notes in exactly the same sequence as the C major scale, but starting from a different point. This is a very important concept for learning modes, because all modes are relative to a primary scale—usually a pure major or pure minor. Because they have been the basis of Western music for so long, the major and minor scales are referred to as **pure scales**. Scales containing exactly the same notes, but with a different starting point, are said to be in a **modal relationship** with a key.

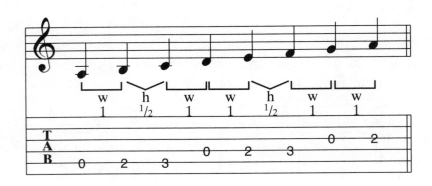

PAPER STRIP MODEL

Think of the notes of a key as being on a long strip of paper, and the scale as being a cardboard template with eight holes in it that the paper passes under. In this case the notes on the paper belong to the key of C.

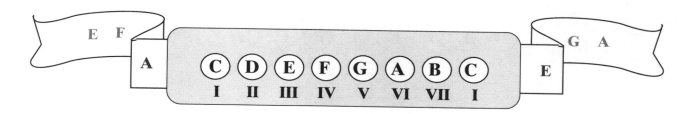

When you pull the paper through the template so that A is in the first position, the A natural minor scale appears.

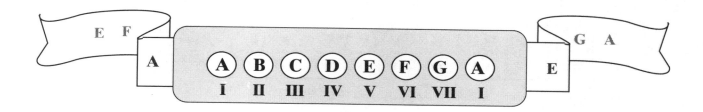

DIFFERENT APPROACHES TO MODES

So far, you have learned that when you take the notes from the key of C and play them in scalar fashion starting on C, you produce a C major scale; when you play the same notes in scalar fashion starting from A, you produce an A natural minor scale. You can use this idea to generate the modes as well. There are also other ways to conceive of modes, and each has a particular advantage, depending on your perspective. Outlined below are several methods for achieving essentially the same result.

The Inversion Approach

The above approach and the paper strip example outline the **Inversion Approach** to modes. The term "inversion" has several different uses in music; in this case, it means playing the same notes in the same sequence, from a different startingpoint.

In the key of C, if you play a "scale" from any note other than C or A, you are playing a **mode**. For example, if you start on D and play all the notes from the C major scale in sequence, no skips, no repeats, until you again reach D—one octave higher than your starting point—you will have played the **Dorian mode.**

Use the paper strip idea to help generate the modes. This is how the D Dorian mode appears:

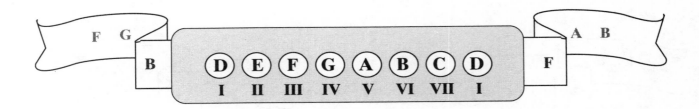

Starting on E and playing the C major scale notes in sequence gives you the **Phrygian mode**.

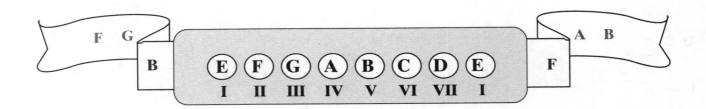

You can use the same technique to generate all the modes. The major and minor scales also have modal names (Ionian and Aeolian), but the term "mode" is usually assigned to scales other than the pure major and pure minor.

Lydian in the Key of C

Mixolydian in the Key of C

Locrian in the Key of C

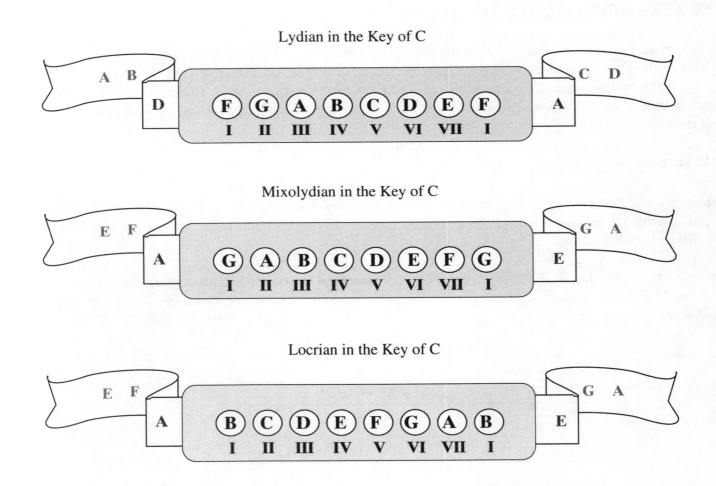

It should now be clear that modes have the same notes as a related major scale, but are played from a different starting point. We still consider C the tonic or "one" (if we are in the key of C), and we simply start on another point in the scale and play seven consecutive ascending steps. There's no need to create a new "tonic." If we changed the tonic, the Dorian mode analysis (numbers indicating scale degrees) would look like this:

When we derive the Dorian mode by "inverting" C major, the analysis is:

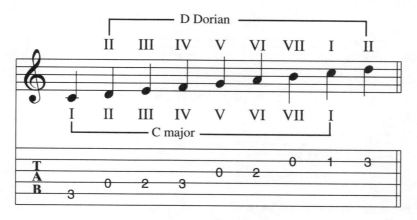

You can think of the Dorian mode as the second mode of C major.
You can find all the other modes using the same process:

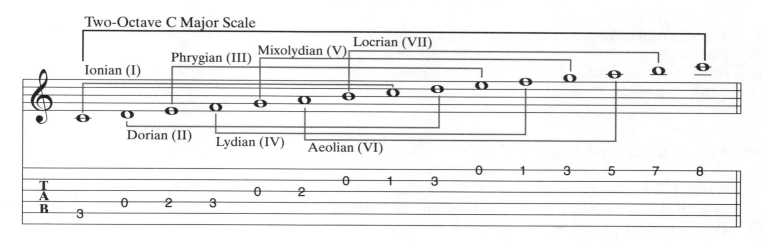

If you know your key signatures well, this is a very quick and effective—although not entirely accurate—way to think of modes. For example, to play E Dorian, you would play from E to E, sharping F and C. This is because the Dorian mode is always the **second** mode of any key. **One** = the tonic (key), so in this case we use the key of D for our available notes, and D has two sharps—F♯ and C♯. This approach involves converting the desired mode to its relative position in the key system and then playing the mode, using the proper accidentals of that key system. It's a bit roundabout, but it's the easiest way to think of modes and most people "play modally" using this approach. The thought process goes something like this: "D Phrygian? That's D to D in the key of B♭—all B's and E's are flat."

■ The Tonic Approach

The way we have generated modes thus far can be thought of as taking the same endless sequence of notes in a given key and merely starting on a note other than the tonic. Remember, though, that the tonic is the home note, the one that all the others are drawn back to, the note that defines the key of a song. To think and play truly modally, you should think of the **mode's** root or starting point as the tonic. A tonic carries with it certain harmonic gravitational properties and cadential tendencies. These properties apply to the mode tonics as well as major and minor scale tonics. The **Tonic Approach** to modes **redefines** the tonic for each mode. This aspect makes the Tonic Approach significantly different from the Inversion Approach: In the Inversion Approach, you play from D to D in the key of C if you want the Dorian mode; D Dorian is the second mode of C. In the Tonic Approach, there is no "key of C," only a tonic D. No reference is made to C in a functional sense; the only connection is that our pitch collection is derived from the key of C (no sharps or flats). D is our anchor or "one." A is our "five," etc. This is the more legitimate way to perceive modes, as each mode is its own entity and is not merely an inversion of a pre-existing major or minor scale.

To illustrate the Tonic Approach to modes, let's start from scratch: Play the D Dorian mode (D to D with no sharps or flats).

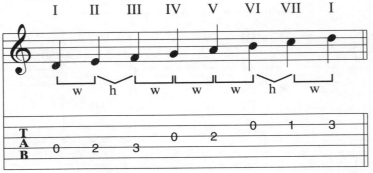

That doesn't have the familiar do-re-mi major scale sound, does it?

- None of the modes has the same sound as the major scale.
- None of the modes sounds like another; each is distinct and unique.

The important concept here is that you are generating the mode by assigning the tonic function to one of the notes in the "key," and then creating a scale by taking the notes in sequence starting from the tonic. In this case, our "key" is D Dorian, defined by our tonic (D) and the sequence of intervals that yields our primary scale—w-h-w-w-w-h-w.

■ Modes As Altered Major or Minor Scales

A third way to think of modes is as altered major or minor scales. That is how modes have come to be thought of as "major" or "minor"—viewing them relative to the scale from which they are derived. For example, the **Dorian mode** can be thought of as a minor scale with a raised (sharped) sixth degree. This gives a "rounder," less classical-sounding minor quality than does the natural minor, and is especially popular in jazz.

The **Phrygian mode** can be thought of as a natural minor scale with a lowered (flatted) second degree. The strange sound of the altered second degree gives this mode an exotic, almost Arabian quality. Metallica is the champion of the Phrygian mode; their songs use the Phrygian mode to create dramatic, eerie musical effects.

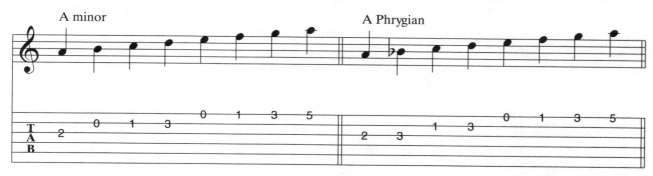

The **Lydian mode** is the major scale with a raised fourth. This mode is the favorite of fusion and progressive players like Steve Vai and Joe Satriani.

The **Mixolydian mode** can be thought of as a major scale with a lowered seventh degree. Many Celtic, Renaissance, and traditional music from the British Isles—and rock music inspired by those styles—use this mode.

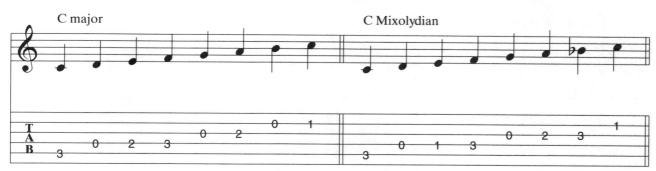

The mode that originates on the sixth degree of the major scale is, of course, the natural minor scale, or the relative minor of the major scale for which the key is named. The modal name for the natural minor scale is the **Aeolian mode**, and compared to its relative major scale, it has a lowered third, sixth and seventh degree. The Aeolian mode is such a universal sound in Western tonal music that it is often not even considered a mode. "God Rest Ye Merry Gentlemen" and "When Johnny Comes Marching Home Again" are examples of songs written in the Aeolian mode.

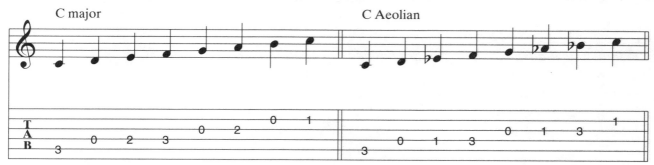

11

The Locrian mode can be thought of as the minor scale with a lowered second and a lowered fifth. Or it could be thought of as the Phrygian mode with a lowered fifth. The relationship between the root and the lowered fifth forms the interval known as the **tritone** (three whole steps). The tritone was once referred to as *diabolus in musica* —the devil in music—and has been shunned by composers and arrangers throughout history. We in the modern age don't attach any "spiritual" or superstitious significance to the tritone, but it remains a difficult and "unmusical" relationship to work with. Consequently, it is hard to find more than passing references to the Locrian mode. Rarely is an entire piece written in this mode—unless, of course, a composer sets out to write a "Locrian mode song" (certainly a valid reason).

To summarize, here is an example showing all the modes compared to the major or minor scale:

Major Scale:	C	D	E	F	G	A	B	C	
Lydian Mode:	C	D	E	**F♯**	G	A	B	C	—Raised 4th
Mixolydian Mode:	C	D	E	F	G	A	**B♭**	C	—Lowered 7th

Minor Scale:	A	B	C	D	E	F	G	A	
Dorian Mode:	A	B	C	D	E	**F♯**	G	A	—Raised 6th
Phrygian Mode:	A	**B♭**	C	D	E	F	G	A	—Lowered 2nd
Locrian Mode:	A	**B♭**	C	D	**E♭**	F	G	A	—Lowered 2nd, —Lowered 5th

Remember, in the common usage of the word, a mode is a special scale that is neither pure major nor pure minor. However, because they are similar to major or minor scales and may be derived by altering major or minor scales, we refer to the individual modes as being either "major" modes or "minor" modes.

- *Ionian, Lydian and Mixolydian are thought of as major modes*

- *Dorian, Phrygian, Locrian and Aeolian are thought of as minor modes*

◼ Modes As Unique Sequences of Intervals

The last way in which to think about modes is to consider each mode as a unique sequence of whole and half steps, without any reference to another scale. This is related to the Tonic Approach to modes but focuses more on the linearity of the specific mode. Knowing the interval structure of each mode would allow you to easily play, for example, consecutive bars of C Lydian, C Dorian, C Locrian, etc. A mode's unique sequence of intervals is what gives it its unique musical "quality" or flavor.

The following descriptions are "intuitive" and are meant to serve only as a general guide to the modes' individual differences, resulting from their unique intervallic makeup.

The Ionian mode (major scale) is formed by a unique sequence of whole and half steps that yields the familiar do-re-mi, etc. sound. It is happy-sounding and triumphant.

$$ C \quad D \quad E \quad F \quad G \quad A \quad B \quad C $$

The Dorian mode's sequence of whole and half steps yields a minor sound with some major qualities. It has a "jazzy" feel:

$$ D \quad E \quad F \quad G \quad A \quad B \quad C \quad D $$

The Phrygian mode's unusual sound at the very beginning of its sequence produces a strange, exotic effect:

$$ E \quad F \quad G \quad A \quad B \quad C \quad D \quad E $$

The Lydian mode has an Impressionistic or "fusion" flavor.

$$ F \quad G \quad A \quad B \quad C \quad D \quad E \quad F $$

The Mixolydian mode sounds major until the very end, when it takes on a "blues" or "dark" quality. It's very effective for producing somber effects without going to a minor mode.

$$ G \quad A \quad B \quad C \quad D \quad E \quad F \quad G $$

The Aeolian (natural minor) mode practically needs no introduction. People describe pieces in this mode as "sad," melancholy," "scary," etc.

$$ A \quad B \quad C \quad D \quad E \quad F \quad G \quad A $$

The Locrian mode doesn't have the intuitive qualities of some of the other more popular modes, but it has been described as "creepy," "foreboding" and "menacing."

$$ B \quad C \quad D \quad E \quad F \quad G \quad A \quad B $$

Thinking of modes as individual entities with unique arrangements of whole- and half-step intervals is a great way for beginning to **think modally**. This will help you to avoid simply playing familiar patterns or falling into "fretboard habits" derived from your approach to the major and minor scales.

PART TWO: USING MODES

Once you understand the way modes are constructed and the individual psycho-musical character of each mode, it's time to apply modes in a musical context.

Modes are usually used as a way of applying melodic ideas over a given set of chord changes. In most songs, analyzing the chord progression will reveal the appropriate mode for those changes. This technique can give you "the right notes" for a guitar solo, and provide a better understanding of the harmonic center of a progression.

DIATONIC TRIADS

For this section we'll return to the major scale. Here again is the pattern of whole and half steps, with the corresponding analysis appearing between the notation and tab:

A **chord** is the simultaneous sounding of three or more notes. A chord has a quality associated with it, such as major, minor, diminished, etc. A **triad** is a three-note chord built in thirds. For example, a C major triad is spelled C, E, G.

A D minor chord is formed with the second, fourth and sixth degrees of C (D, F, A):

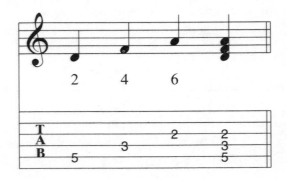

If we applied this pattern to each note on the scale, we would get the following chords:

The three notes in any triad are called the **root, third** and **fifth**; the first note is always the root. For example, the triad on C uses the first, third and fifth notes of the scale:

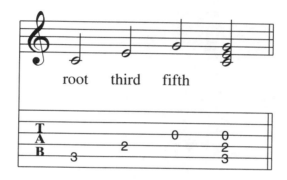

root   third   fifth

The triad starting on the second note of the scale uses the second, fourth and sixth notes of C, but when speaking of the D minor **chord**, the notes are called the root, third and fifth:

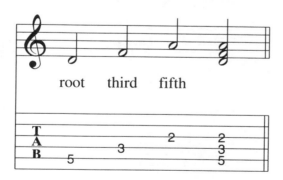

root   third   fifth

Such chords, derived from a major scale, are called **diatonic triads.** Upon listening to these triads, you will find that there are three qualities of diatonic triads.

Major triads occur on degrees I, IV and V (C, F and G):

Minor triads occur on degrees II, III and VI (D, E and A):

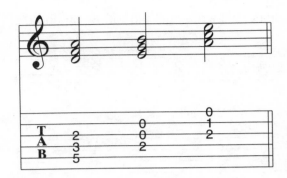

The **Diminished** triad falls on degree VII (B):

Let's look at the differences between these three kinds of triads.

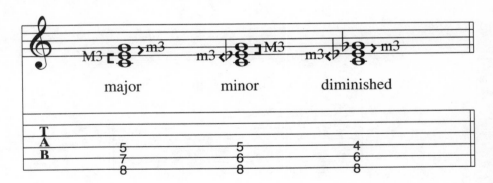

The only difference between major and minor triads is that the **third** (the middle note) is a half step closer to the root in the minor triad than in the major. In a major triad the third is two whole steps away from the root; a minor triad's third is one and a half steps away from the root. Thus, a major third is two whole steps apart and a minor third is one and a half steps apart.

- *A major triad consists of a major third and a minor third*

- *A minor triad consists of a minor third and a major third*

- *A diminished triad consists of two minor thirds*

The ability to identify chords as major, minor or diminished is important in determining a song's key or mode. To differentiate between chord qualities, major chords will be indicated in upper-case Roman numerals, minor chords in lower-case Roman numerals, and diminished chords in lower-case Roman numerals with the diminished sign (°) added. The triad's diatonic location and quality can then be referred to by number. For example, in C major, you could call the following chords D minor, G major and C major:

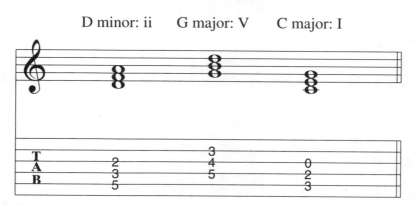

Or you could refer to them as ii, V and I of C.

Returning now to our diatonic triads, we find:

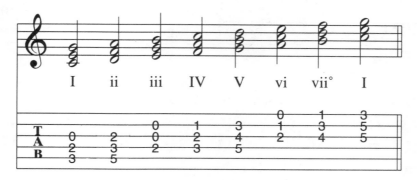

By taking any major scale and forming triads this way, the same pattern will result. Here is the pattern in G (remember, the F's must be sharped to yield the correct results):

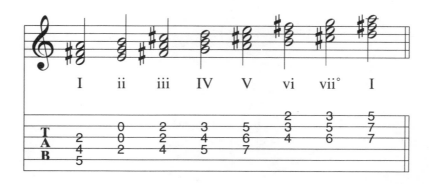

Here are the diatonic triads in D (F♯ and C♯ are the accidentals):

The diatonic triads work the same way for every major scale.

In any major scale: I, IV and V are major
                       ii, iii and vi are minor
                       vii° is diminished

THE RELATIVE MINOR SCALE

We have learned that when we take the notes from the C major scale and play them in scalar fashion (alphabetically) starting from the sixth note of the scale (A), we get the **A natural minor scale**, and that this scale is also called the **relative minor scale** for C major because it contains exactly the same notes. Using the Tonic Approach to modes, let's name A as our new tonic.

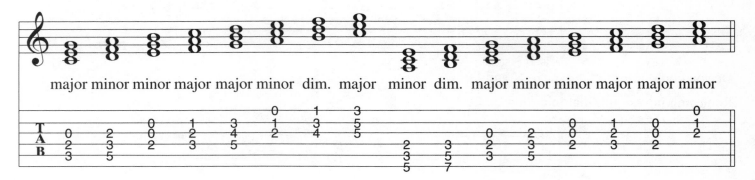

major minor minor major major minor dim. major minor dim. major minor minor major major minor

If A is now our new tonic (or I), what does that do to our diatonic triads? Compare C major to A natural minor:

C D   E   F   G   A   B   C   A   B   C   D   E   F   G   A
I ii iii IV V   vi vii° I   i   ii° III iv v   VI VII i

In both scales the letter names have the same chord qualities (A, D and E are minor, etc.) but their relationship to the tonic has changed; the numerical assignments (function) are different.

THE FLOATING WHEEL CONCEPT

Visualizing these chords may help you to better understand the concept of changing functions. Imagine you have a plastic wheel with the chord symbols on it:

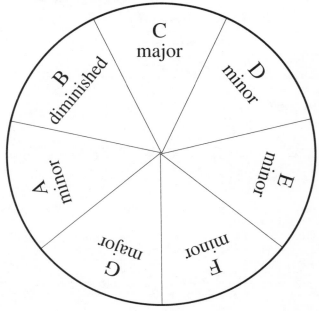

Pretend also that this wheel floats in water, but only the top seventh of the wheel is visible above the water.

Depending on which chord is on top, you might think of the wheel as a C major wheel…

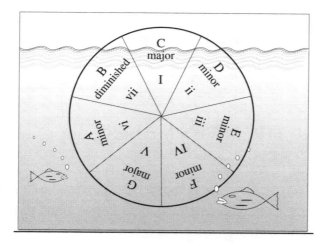

…or an A minor wheel:

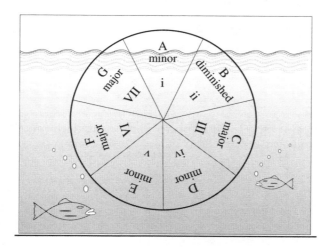

Yet **nothing on the wheel has changed**. The distance from one chord to another remains exactly the same and the order of the chords is the same. The only difference is how you look at it, and which chord you use as the starting point (one). This concept applies to all major and relative minor scales, and relative modes.

Remember, the tonic is like a magnet, always pulling the music back toward itself. The last chord of most songs is the tonic.

Looking at the C major and A minor scales, we see that while the chord letter-names and qualities are the same (e.g., the D chord is minor in both scales), the tonic is different. A song in C major will pull the progression back toward the C major triad:

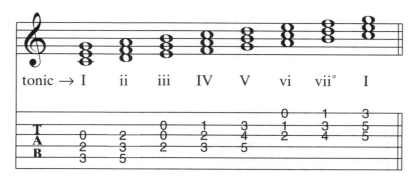

A song in A minor will lead back toward the A minor triad:

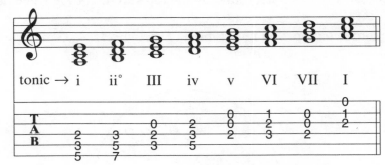

tonic → i   ii°   III   iv   v   VI   VII   I

THE DIATONIC SCALE AND THE SEVEN MODES

Let's look at the seven modes and how they relate to the diatonic triads. Since several different modes can legally operate in the same key (for example, D Dorian and A Aeolian), we need to analyze the **chord progression** to determine which chord is acting as the tonic. How do you know which mode you are in if the chord qualities among related modes are all the same?

The answer: *Each mode has characteristic chord progressions that define the tonic.*

Let's consider the modes generated by the key of C and their relationship to the diatonic chords of the C major scale. These relationships are true of any major scale and its related modes.

Ionian Mode

The major scale is also a mode. It is called the **Ionian mode**. Here is its defining chord progression:

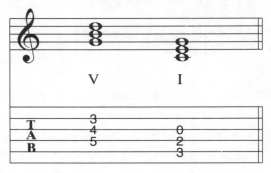

V   I

The V-I progression almost always leads you to the tonic, which dictates the Ionian mode. An even stronger resolution is the V7-to-I progression, which produces a **cadence**:

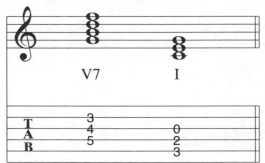

V7   I

The fifth degree in any major scale (G in C major, for example) is the only note on which a dominant-seventh chord naturally occurs. Dominant-sevenths, like triads, use an every-other-note pattern. Notice that the seventh in this chord is three half steps above the fifth of the chord. The progression G7 to C strongly pulls the harmonic progression back to C. Any time you hear such a progression (V7-I or V-I), you are in the Ionian mode (major scale).

Here are three examples of chord progressions that imply the Ionian mode:

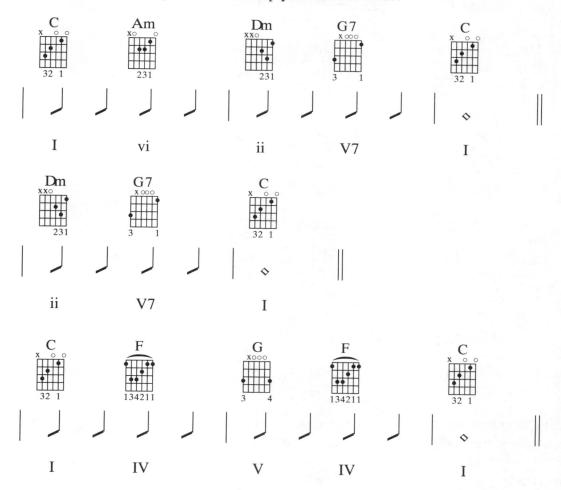

Watch out for progressions like this:

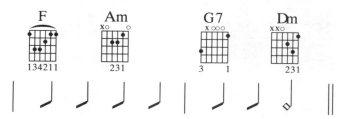

This one appears to be in C major, but ends up elsewhere. D is the tonic. A progression where a dominant-seventh chord doesn't resolve to its apparent tonic (in this case G7 does not resolve to C) is called a **deceptive cadence**. It intentionally goes against the V7-to-I tendency.

■ Dorian Mode

The Dorian mode is made by treating the second degree of a major scale as the tonic. Here are the triads from its harmonized scale:

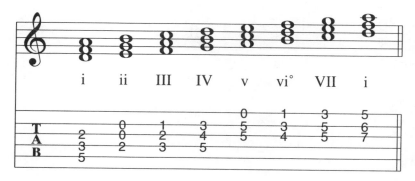

Here are two characteristic Dorian progressions:

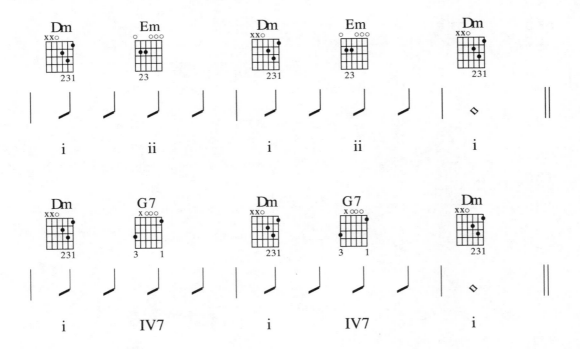

Remember, to identify a mode, you must be able to identify the tonic. Both of the above examples end on D minor. (Most songs, especially modal songs, end on the tonic.)

Phrygian Mode

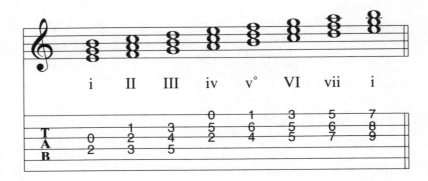

The mode that begins on the third degree of a major scale is the Phrygian.

Here is its characteristic progression:

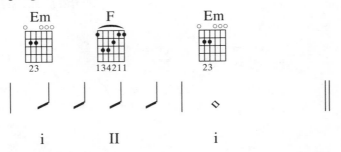

22

Lydian Mode

The mode that starts on the fourth degree is the Lydian.

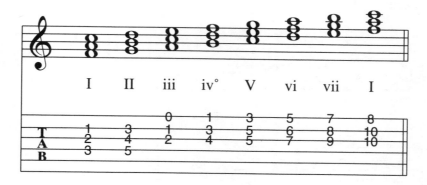

Its characteristic progression is:

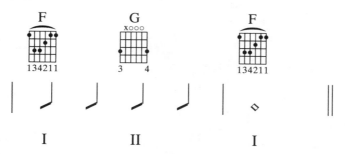

Mixolydian Mode

The Mixolydian mode starts on the fifth degree.

Its characteristic progression is:

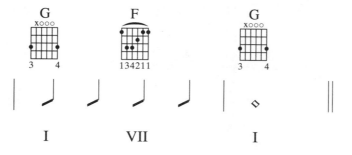

Warning: Two adjacent major chords can imply either Lydian or Mixolydian, so double-check the tonic. Listen carefully until you are certain which chord the progression ends on or resolves to.

■ Aeolian Mode

The natural minor mode, Aeolian, starts on the sixth note of the major scale.

Its characteristic progressions are:

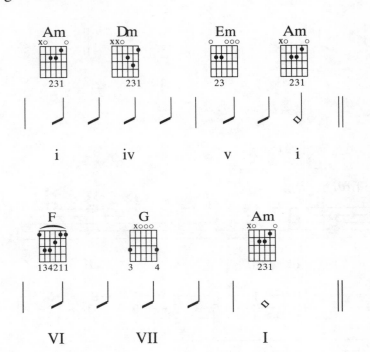

■ Locrian Mode

The last mode, Locrian, is made by starting on the seventh step of the major scale.

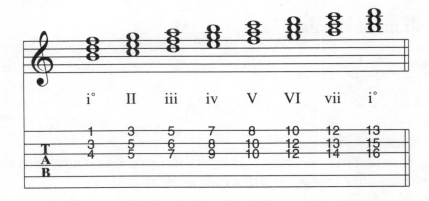

Its identifying chord is the minor-seven flat-five or half-diminished chord.

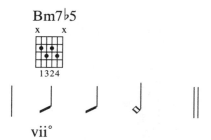

PENTATONIC SCALES and MODES

Rarely is a song entirely in one mode. Just as songs that use only the notes of C major are rather colorless, songs employing only one mode are harmonically limiting. Modes tend to appear in **passages**—sections of music occurring within a smaller harmonic framework, usually defined by a sequence of chords. This results in "temporary tonics," "momentary modulations" or short-term harmonic centers that require the player to switch quickly between modal lead patterns. With accomplished players, the smoothness and integrity of the melodic line remains intact, regardless of the shifting key centers. To use modal playing successfully, you must be able to hit the "right notes" without compromising your melodic inspirations; you must strive to switch between the modes quickly and seamlessly.

In this section we will learn the modal lead patterns that occur within a basic pentatonic minor scale pattern. You have already learned that the pentatonic scale is a great way to begin soloing; virtually every note in the scale sounds good over any chord. The pentatonic scale gets your fingers moving and your ears working without worrying about scales, theory, etc. Stay within the pentatonic scale and you'll never play a "wrong" note.

The modes have pentatonic versions that accomplish the same goal. The modal pentatonics allow you to capture the flavor of the complete versions of the modes while guaranteeing no wrong notes. And, like its "rock box" counterpart, each pattern satisfies two modes.

Here, for review, is the A minor pentatonic scale in fifth position. This scale fits over songs in A minor or C major.

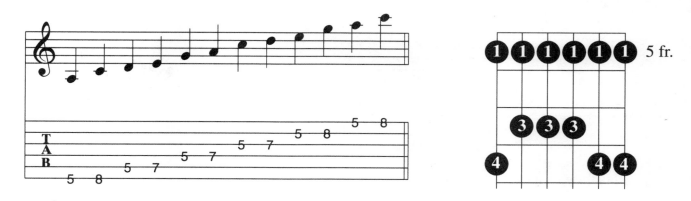

Remember, C major and A minor contain the same notes, so all the notes in the A minor pentatonic scale (which is an A natural minor scale minus two notes) are also notes in the C major scale. So if you want to improvise in the key of C major, you can play the A minor pentatonic scale without a hitch.

There are three modal pairs that use this idea.

◼ Aeolian/Ionian

You can play the A minor pentatonic scale for songs in A minor (Aeolian) or C major (Ionian).

Here is a chord progression in A minor:

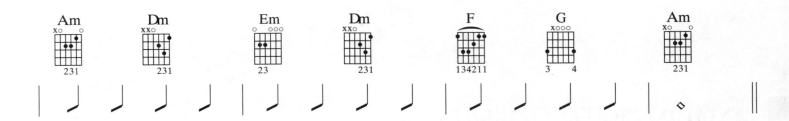

Here is a chord progression in C major. Record these chord progressions into a tape recorder and practice playing your A minor pentatonic scale against them.

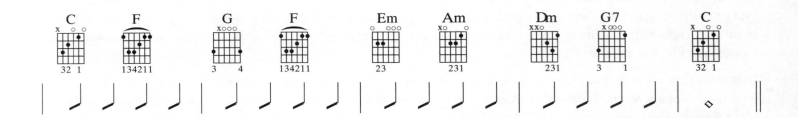

◼ Dorian/Lydian

Here is the pentatonic pattern for Dorian or Lydian:

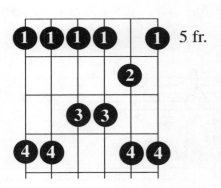

You can use this for passages in D Dorian:

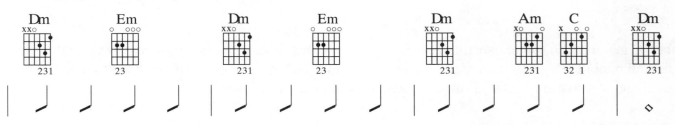

26

Or passages in F Lydian:

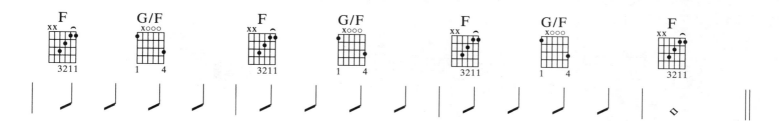

Phrygian/Mixolydian

Here is the pattern for Phrygian or Mixolydian:

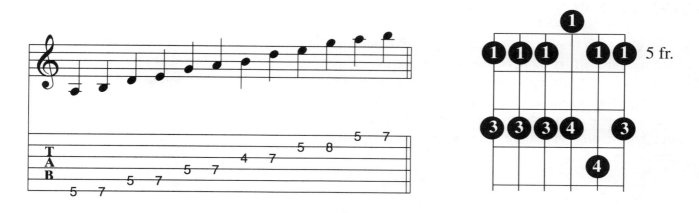

You can use this for passages in E Phrygian:

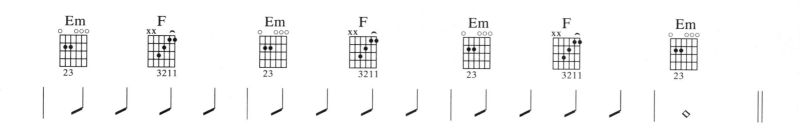

Or passages in G Mixolydian.

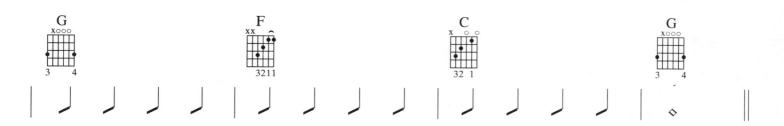

Locrian

There really is no pentatonic pattern for the Locrian mode, but here is a four-note pattern that covers Locrian-based chords, such as Bm7♭5.

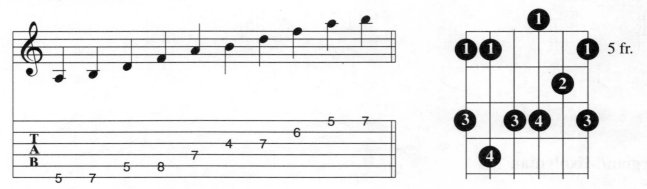

RELATIVE PENTATONICS

We have learned to play a pentatonic scale in three different places, each of which works with two modes. But wait a minute! All six modes are comprised of the same notes and chords. Shouldn't all three pentatonics work with any mode? Well, yes—but you must be careful. The pentatonic-to-mode relationships given earlier are the ones that *always* work. If you play a pentatonic designed for one mode pair (such as Aeolian/Ionian) against a progression that outlines a different mode (such as Mixolydian), you will sometimes find notes that don't work with all the chords, and dissonance will result. For example, this passage, using the Aeolian/Ionian pattern, sounds fine:

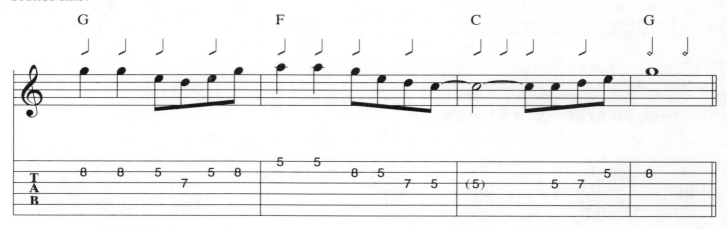

But this passage—using the same pentatonic pattern with the same chord progression—sounds wrong:

The A minor pentatonic blends well with almost all chords in the key. The modal pentatonics will work fine when used with chord progressions they were designed for, but not always with chords that outline another mode. Here, you must be careful about your choice of notes. To avoid musical messes, experiment with different combinations of notes and chords to see what works. Once that's settled, you can play all three pentatonics for any of the seven modes.

In other words, if you are playing lead for a song in any of these modes:

C IONIAN (major)
D DORIAN
E PHRYGIAN
F LYDIAN
G MIXOLYDIAN
A AEOLIAN (natural minor)
B LOCRIAN

You could solo successfully out of any of these pentatonics—if you are careful of your note choices:

A AEOLIAN
D DORIAN
E PHRYGIAN

So far we have studied seven modes, their identifying chord progressions, and some ways to solo over them. For simplicity's sake, we have restricted ourselves to modes that use the notes in the C major scale. Remember, there are 11 other major keys, and each is the "parent" to seven related modes.

To expand your musicianship, try identifying and soloing over songs in other key families. A key family is the group of seven modes that relate to a particular major or minor key. For example, the G major key family consists of:

G IONIAN (major)
A DORIAN
B PHRYGIAN
C LYDIAN
D MIXOLYDIAN
E AEOLIAN (natural minor)
F♯ LOCRIAN

Identify the following progressions; then answer these questions:

     1. What mode is it in?
     2. To what key family does it belong?
     3. Which three pentatonics can I play with this progression?

Ex.1

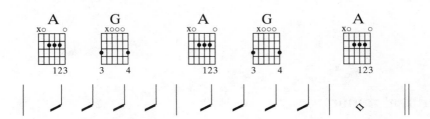

Ex. 2

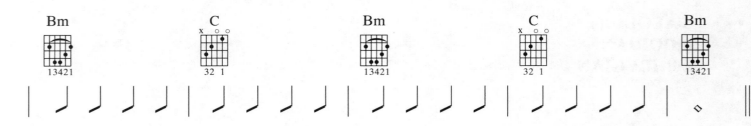

Ex. 3

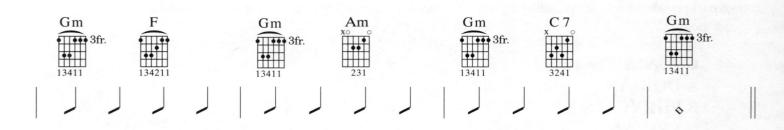

Ex. 4

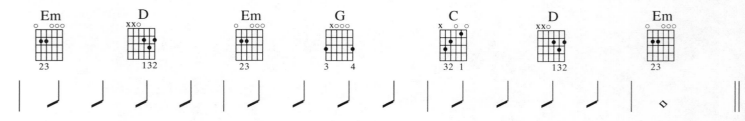

Answers:

Ex.1   Mode: A Mixolydian
         Key: D major key family
         Pentatonics: B minor pentatonic, E minor pentatonic, F♯ minor pentatonic

Ex. 2 Mode: B Phrygian
         Key: G major key family
         Pentatonics: E minor pentatonic, A minor pentatonic, B minor pentatonic

Ex. 3 Mode: G Dorian
         Key: F major key family
         Pentatonics: D minor pentatonic, G minor pentatonic, A minor pentatonic

Ex. 4 Mode: E Aeolian
                        Key: G major key family
                        Pentatonics: E minor pentatonic, A minor pentatonic, B minor pentatonic

Conclusion

You should now be able to identify a song's mode from its chord progression. You should also be able to solo over it in three pentatonic positions. This is the beginning of modal metal guitar the way Vai, Satriani, Slash, Hammett and other rock greats play it. The next step is to fill in the two missing notes of the pentatonics to make complete modes, and to play out of major and minor scale positions. For now, though, have fun—and keep rockin'!

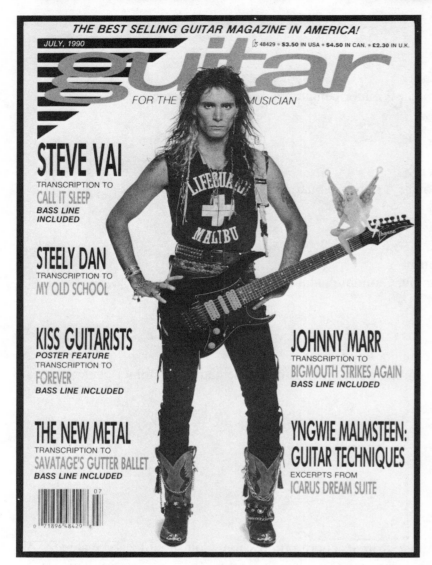